The Poetry of Henry Wadsworth Longfellow

Volume II – The Belfry of Bruges & Other Poems

Henry Wadsworth Longfellow was born on February 27th, 1807 in Portland, Maine. As a young boy, it was obvious that he was very studious and he quickly became fluent in Latin.

He published his first poem, "The Battle of Lovell's Pond", in the Portland Gazette on November 17th, 1820. He was already thinking of a career in literature and, in his senior year, wrote to his father: "I will not disguise it in the least... the fact is, I most eagerly aspire after future eminence in literature, my whole soul burns most ardently after it, and every earthly thought centers in it...."

After graduation travels in Europe occupied the next three years and he seemed to easily absorb any language he set himself to learn.

On September 14th, 1831, Longfellow married Mary Storer Potter. They settled in Brunswick.

His first published book was in 1833, a translation of poems by the Spanish poet Jorge Manrique. He also published a travel book, Outre-Mer: A Pilgrimage Beyond the Sea.

During a trip to Europe Mary became pregnant. Sadly, in October 1835, she miscarried at some six months. After weeks of illness she died, at the age of 22 on November 29th, 1835. Longfellow wrote "One thought occupies me night and day... She is dead — She is dead! All day I am weary and sad".

In late 1839, Longfellow published Hyperion, a book in prose inspired by his trips abroad.

Ballads and Other Poems was published in 1841 and included "The Village Blacksmith" and "The Wreck of the Hesperus". His reputation as a poet, and a commercial one at that, was set.

On May 10th, 1843, after seven years in pursuit of a chance for new love, Longfellow received word from Fanny Appleton that she agreed to marry him.

On November 1st, 1847, the epic poem Evangeline was published.

In 1854, Longfellow retired from Harvard, to devote himself entirely to writing.

The Song of Haiwatha, perhaps his best known and enjoyed work was published in 1855.

On July 10th, 1861, after suffering horrific burns the previous day. In his attempts to save her Longfellow had also been badly burned and was unable to attend her funeral.

He spent several years translating Dante Alighieri's Divine Comedy. It was published in 1867.

Longfellow was also part of a group who became known as The Fireside Poets which also included William Cullen Bryant, John Greenleaf Whittier, James Russell Lowell, and Oliver Wendell Holmes Snr.

Longfellow was the most popular poet of his day. As a friend once wrote to him, "no other poet was so fully recognized in his lifetime". Some of his works including "Paul Revere's Ride" and "The Song of Haiwatha" may have rewritten the facts but became essential parts of the American psyche and culture.

Henry Wadsworth Longfellow died, surrounded by family, on Friday, March 24th, 1882. He had been suffering from peritonitis.

Index of Contents

THE BELFRY OF BRUGES AND OTHER POEMS

THE BELFRY OF BRUGES
CARILLON

In the ancient town of Bruges,
In the quaint old Flemish city,
As the evening shades descended,
Low and loud and sweetly blended,
Low at times and loud at times,
And changing like a poet's rhymes,
Rang the beautiful wild chimes
From the Belfry in the market
Of the ancient town of Bruges.

Then, with deep sonorous clangor
Calmly answering their sweet anger,
When the wrangling bells had ended,
Slowly struck the clock eleven,
And, from out the silent heaven,
Silence on the town descended.
Silence, silence everywhere,
On the earth and in the air,
Save that footsteps here and there
Of some burgher home returning,
By the street lamps faintly burning,
For a moment woke the echoes
Of the ancient town of Bruges.

But amid my broken slumbers
Still I heard those magic numbers,
As they loud proclaimed the flight
And stolen marches of the night;
Till their chimes in sweet collision
Mingled with each wandering vision,
Mingled with the fortune-telling
Gypsy-bands of dreams and fancies,
Which amid the waste expanses
Of the silent land of trances
Have their solitary dwelling;
All else seemed asleep in Bruges,
In the quaint old Flemish city.

And I thought how like these chimes
Are the poet's airy rhymes,
All his rhymes and roundelays,
His conceits, and songs, and ditties,
From the belfry of his brain,
Scattered downward, though in vain,
On the roofs and stones of cities!
For by night the drowsy ear
Under its curtains cannot hear,
And by day men go their ways,

Hearing the music as they pass,
But deeming it no more, alas!
Than the hollow sound of brass.

Yet perchance a sleepless wight,
Lodging at some humble inn
In the narrow lanes of life,
When the dusk and hush of night
Shut out the incessant din
Of daylight and its toil and strife,
May listen with a calm delight
To the poet's melodies,
Till he hears, or dreams he hears,
Intermingled with the song,
Thoughts that he has cherished long;
Hears amid the chime and singing
The bells of his own village ringing,
And wakes, and finds his slumberous eyes
Wet with most delicious tears.

Thus dreamed I, as by night I lay
In Bruges, at the Fleur-de-Ble,
Listening with a wild delight
To the chimes that, through the night
Bang their changes from the Belfry
Of that quaint old Flemish city.

THE BELFRY OF BRUGES

In the market-place of Bruges stands the belfry old and brown;
Thrice consumed and thrice rebuilded, still it watches o'er the town.

As the summer morn was breaking, on that lofty tower I stood,
And the world threw off the darkness, like the weeds of widowhood.

Thick with towns and hamlets studded, and with streams and vapors gray,
Like a shield embossed with silver, round and vast the landscape lay.

At my feet the city slumbered. From its chimneys, here and there,
Wreaths of snow-white smoke, ascending, vanished, ghost-like, into air.

Not a sound rose from the city at that early morning hour,
But I heard a heart of iron beating in the ancient tower.

From their nests beneath the rafters sang the swallows wild and high;
And the world, beneath me sleeping, seemed more distant than the sky.

Then most musical and solemn, bringing back the olden times,
With their strange, unearthly changes rang the melancholy chimes,

Like the psalms from some old cloister, when the nuns sing in the choir;
And the great bell tolled among them, like the chanting of a friar.

Visions of the days departed, shadowy phantoms filled my brain;
They who live in history only seemed to walk the earth again;

All the Foresters of Flanders,—mighty Baldwin Bras de Fer,
Lyderick du Bucq and Cressy Philip, Guy de Dampierre.

I beheld the pageants splendid that adorned those days of old;
Stately dames, like queens attended, knights who bore the Fleece of Gold

Lombard and Venetian merchants with deep-laden argosies;
Ministers from twenty nations; more than royal pomp and ease.

I beheld proud Maximilian, kneeling humbly on the ground;
I beheld the gentle Mary, hunting with her hawk and hound;

And her lighted bridal-chamber, where a duke slept with the queen,
And the armed guard around them, and the sword unsheathed between.

I beheld the Flemish weavers, with Namur and Juliers bold,
Marching homeward from the bloody battle of the Spurs of Gold;

Saw the light at Minnewater, saw the White Hoods moving west,
Saw great Artevelde victorious scale the Golden Dragon's nest.

And again the whiskered Spaniard all the land with terror smote;
And again the wild alarum sounded from the tocsin's throat;

Till the bell of Ghent responded o'er lagoon and dike of sand,
"I am Roland! I am Roland! there is victory in the land!"

Then the sound of drums aroused me. The awakened city's roar
Chased the phantoms I had summoned back into their graves once more.

Hours had passed away like minutes; and, before I was aware,
Lo! the shadow of the belfry crossed the sun-illumined square.

A GLEAM OF SUNSHINE

This is the place. Stand still, my steed,

Let me review the scene,
And summon from the shadowy Past
The forms that once have been.

The Past and Present here unite
Beneath Time's flowing tide,
Like footprints hidden by a brook,
But seen on either side.

Here runs the highway to the town;
There the green lane descends,
Through which I walked to church with thee,
O gentlest of my friends!

The shadow of the linden-trees
Lay moving on the grass;
Between them and the moving boughs,
A shadow, thou didst pass.

Thy dress was like the lilies,
And thy heart as pure as they:
One of God's holy messengers
Did walk with me that day.

I saw the branches of the trees
Bend down thy touch to meet,
The clover-blossoms in the grass
Rise up to kiss thy feet,

"Sleep, sleep to-day, tormenting cares,
Of earth and folly born!"
Solemnly sang the village choir
On that sweet Sabbath morn.

Through the closed blinds the golden sun
Poured in a dusty beam,
Like the celestial ladder seen
By Jacob in his dream.

And ever and anon, the wind,
Sweet-scented with the hay,
Turned o'er the hymn-book's fluttering leaves
That on the window lay.

Long was the good man's sermon,
Yet it seemed not so to me;
For he spake of Ruth the beautiful,
And still I thought of thee.

Long was the prayer he uttered,
Yet it seemed not so to me;
For in my heart I prayed with him,
And still I thought of thee.

But now, alas! the place seems changed;
Thou art no longer here:
Part of the sunshine of the scene
With thee did disappear.

Though thoughts, deep-rooted in my heart,
Like pine-trees dark and high,
Subdue the light of noon, and breathe
A low and ceaseless sigh;

This memory brightens o'er the past,
As when the sun, concealed
Behind some cloud that near us hangs
Shines on a distant field.

THE ARSENAL AT SPRINGFIELD

This is the Arsenal. From floor to ceiling,
Like a huge organ, rise the burnished arms;
But front their silent pipes no anthem pealing
Startles the villages with strange alarms.

Ah! what a sound will rise, how wild and dreary,
When the death-angel touches those swift keys
What loud lament and dismal Miserere
Will mingle with their awful symphonies

I hear even now the infinite fierce chorus,
The cries of agony, the endless groan,
Which, through the ages that have gone before us,
In long reverberations reach our own.

On helm and harness rings the Saxon hammer,
Through Cimbric forest roars the Norseman's song,
And loud, amid the universal clamor,
O'er distant deserts sounds the Tartar gong.

I hear the Florentine, who from his palace
Wheels out his battle-bell with dreadful din,
And Aztec priests upon their teocallis

Beat the wild war-drums made of serpent's skin;

The tumult of each sacked and burning village;
The shout that every prayer for mercy drowns;
The soldiers' revels in the midst of pillage;
The wail of famine in beleaguered towns;

The bursting shell, the gateway wrenched asunder,
The rattling musketry, the clashing blade;
And ever and anon, in tones of thunder,
The diapason of the cannonade.

Is it, O man, with such discordant noises,
With such accursed instruments as these,
Thou drownest Nature's sweet and kindly voices,
And jarrest the celestial harmonies?

Were half the power, that fills the world with terror,
Were half the wealth, bestowed on camps and courts,
Given to redeem the human mind from error,
There were no need of arsenals or forts:

The warrior's name would be a name abhorred!
And every nation, that should lift again
Its hand against a brother, on its forehead
Would wear forevermore the curse of Cain!

Down the dark future, through long generations,
The echoing sounds grow fainter and then cease;
And like a bell, with solemn, sweet vibrations,
I hear once more the voice of Christ say, "Peace!"

Peace! and no longer from its brazen portals
The blast of War's great organ shakes the skies!
But beautiful as songs of the immortals,
The holy melodies of love arise.

NUREMBERG

In the valley of the Pegnitz, where across broad meadow-lands
Rise the blue Franconian mountains, Nuremberg, the ancient, stands.

Quaint old town of toil and traffic, quaint old town of art and song,
Memories haunt thy pointed gables, like the rooks that round them throng:

Memories of the Middle Ages, when the emperors, rough and bold,

Had their dwelling in thy castle, time-defying, centuries old;

And thy brave and thrifty burghers boasted, in their uncouth rhyme,
That their great imperial city stretched its hand through every clime.

In the court-yard of the castle, bound with many an iron hand,
Stands the mighty linden planted by Queen Cunigunde's hand;

On the square the oriel window, where in old heroic days
Sat the poet Melchior singing Kaiser Maximilian's praise.

Everywhere I see around me rise the wondrous world of Art:
Fountains wrought with richest sculpture standing in the common mart;

And above cathedral doorways saints and bishops carved in stone,
By a former age commissioned as apostles to our own.

In the church of sainted Sebald sleeps enshrined his holy dust,
And in bronze the Twelve Apostles guard from age to age their trust;

In the church of sainted Lawrence stands a pix of sculpture rare,
Like the foamy sheaf of fountains, rising through the painted air.

Here, when Art was still religion, with a simple, reverent heart,
Lived and labored Albrecht Durer, the Evangelist of Art;

Hence in silence and in sorrow, toiling still with busy hand,
Like an emigrant he wandered, seeking for the Better Land.

Emigravit is the inscription on the tombstone where he lies;
Dead he is not, but departed,—for the artist never dies.

Fairer seems the ancient city, and the sunshine seems more fair,
That he once has trod its pavement, that he once has breathed its air!

Through these streets so broad and stately, these obscure and dismal lanes,
Walked of yore the Mastersingers, chanting rude poetic strains.

From remote and sunless suburbs came they to the friendly guild,
Building nests in Fame's great temple, as in spouts the swallows build.

As the weaver plied the shuttle, wove he too the mystic rhyme,
And the smith his iron measures hammered to the anvil's chime;

Thanking God, whose boundless wisdom makes the flowers of poesy bloom
In the forge's dust and cinders, in the tissues of the loom.

Here Hans Sachs, the cobbler-poet, laureate of the gentle craft,

Wisest of the Twelve Wise Masters, in huge folios sang and laughed.

But his house is now an ale-house, with a nicely sanded floor,
And a garland in the window, and his face above the door;

Painted by some humble artist, as in Adam Puschman's song,
As the old man gray and dove-like, with his great beard white and long.

And at night the swart mechanic comes to drown his cark and care,
Quaffing ale from pewter tankard; in the master's antique chair.

Vanished is the ancient splendor, and before my dreamy eye
Wave these mingled shapes and figures, like a faded tapestry.

Not thy Councils, not thy Kaisers, win for thee the world's regard;
But thy painter, Albrecht Durer, and Hans Sachs thy cobbler-bard.

Thus, O Nuremberg, a wanderer from a region far away,
As he paced thy streets and court-yards, sang in thought his careless lay:

Gathering from the pavement's crevice, as a floweret of the soil,
The nobility of labor,—the long pedigree of toil.

THE NORMAN BARON

*Dans les moments de la vie ou la reflexion devient plus calme et plus profonde, ou l'interet et l'avarice parlent moins haut que la raison, dans les instants de chagrin domestique, de maladie, et de peril de mort, les nobles se repentirent de posseder des serfs, comme d'une chose peu agreable a Dieu, qui avait cree tous les hommes a son image.—**THIERRY**, Conquete de l'Angleterre.*

In his chamber, weak and dying,
Was the Norman baron lying;
Loud, without, the tempest thundered
And the castle-turret shook,

In this fight was Death the gainer,
Spite of vassal and retainer,
And the lands his sires had plundered,
Written in the Doomsday Book.

By his bed a monk was seated,
Who in humble voice repeated
Many a prayer and pater-noster,
From the missal on his knee;

And, amid the tempest pealing,

Sounds of bells came faintly stealing,
Bells, that from the neighboring kloster
Rang for the Nativity.

In the hall, the serf and vassal
Held, that night their Christmas wassail;
Many a carol, old and saintly,
Sang the minstrels and the waits;

And so loud these Saxon gleemen
Sang to slaves the songs of freemen,
That the storm was heard but faintly,
Knocking at the castle-gates.

Till at length the lays they chanted
Reached the chamber terror-haunted,
Where the monk, with accents holy,
Whispered at the baron's ear.

Tears upon his eyelids glistened,
As he paused awhile and listened,
And the dying baron slowly
Turned his weary head to hear.

"Wassail for the kingly stranger
Born and cradled in a manger!
King, like David, priest, like Aaron,
Christ is born to set us free!"

And the lightning showed the sainted
Figures on the casement painted,
And exclaimed the shuddering baron,
"Miserere, Domine!"

In that hour of deep contrition
He beheld, with clearer vision,
Through all outward show and fashion,
Justice, the Avenger, rise.

All the pomp of earth had vanished,
Falsehood and deceit were banished,
Reason spake more loud than passion,
And the truth wore no disguise.

Every vassal of his banner,
Every serf born to his manor,
All those wronged and wretched creatures,
By his hand were freed again.

And, as on the sacred missal
He recorded their dismissal,
Death relaxed his iron features,
And the monk replied, "Amen!"

Many centuries have been numbered
Since in death the baron slumbered
By the convent's sculptured portal,
Mingling with the common dust:

But the good deed, through the ages
Living in historic pages,
Brighter grows and gleams immortal,
Unconsumed by moth or rust

RAIN IN SUMMER

How beautiful is the rain!
After the dust and heat,
In the broad and fiery street,
In the narrow lane,
How beautiful is the rain!

How it clatters along the roofs,
Like the tramp of hoofs
How it gushes and struggles out
From the throat of the overflowing spout!

Across the window-pane
It pours and pours;
And swift and wide,
With a muddy tide,
Like a river down the gutter roars
The rain, the welcome rain!

The sick man from his chamber looks
At the twisted brooks;
He can feel the cool
Breath of each little pool;
His fevered brain
Grows calm again,
And he breathes a blessing on the rain.

From the neighboring school
Come the boys,

With more than their wonted noise
And commotion;
And down the wet streets
Sail their mimic fleets,
Till the treacherous pool
Ingulfs them in its whirling
And turbulent ocean.

In the country, on every side,
Where far and wide,
Like a leopard's tawny and spotted hide,
Stretches the plain,
To the dry grass and the drier grain
How welcome is the rain!

In the furrowed land
The toilsome and patient oxen stand;
Lifting the yoke encumbered head,
With their dilated nostrils spread,
They silently inhale
The clover-scented gale,
And the vapors that arise
From the well-watered and smoking soil.
For this rest in the furrow after toil
Their large and lustrous eyes
Seem to thank the Lord,
More than man's spoken word.

Near at hand,
From under the sheltering trees,
The farmer sees
His pastures, and his fields of grain,
As they bend their tops
To the numberless beating drops
Of the incessant rain.
He counts it as no sin
That he sees therein
Only his own thrift and gain.

These, and far more than these,
The Poet sees!
He can behold
Aquarius old
Walking the fenceless fields of air;
And from each ample fold
Of the clouds about him rolled
Scattering everywhere
The showery rain,

As the farmer scatters his grain.

He can behold
Things manifold
That have not yet been wholly told,—
Have not been wholly sung nor said.
For his thought, that never stops,
Follows the water-drops
Down to the graves of the dead,
Down through chasms and gulfs profound,
To the dreary fountain-head
Of lakes and rivers under ground;
And sees them, when the rain is done,
On the bridge of colors seven
Climbing up once more to heaven,
Opposite the setting sun.

Thus the Seer,
With vision clear,
Sees forms appear and disappear,
In the perpetual round of strange,
Mysterious change
From birth to death, from death to birth,
From earth to heaven, from heaven to earth;
Till glimpses more sublime
Of things, unseen before,
Unto his wondering eyes reveal
The Universe, as an immeasurable wheel
Turning forevermore
In the rapid and rushing river of Time.

TO A CHILD

Dear child! how radiant on thy mother's knee,
With merry-making eyes and jocund smiles,
Thou gazest at the painted tiles,
Whose figures grace,
With many a grotesque form and face.
The ancient chimney of thy nursery!
The lady with the gay macaw,
The dancing girl, the grave bashaw
With bearded lip and chin;
And, leaning idly o'er his gate,
Beneath the imperial fan of state,
The Chinese mandarin.

With what a look of proud command
Thou shakest in thy little hand
The coral rattle with its silver bells,
Making a merry tune!
Thousands of years in Indian seas
That coral grew, by slow degrees,
Until some deadly and wild monsoon
Dashed it on Coromandel's sand!
Those silver bells
Reposed of yore,
As shapeless ore,
Far down in the deep-sunken wells
Of darksome mines,
In some obscure and sunless place,
Beneath huge Chimborazo's base,
Or Potosi's o'erhanging pines
And thus for thee, O little child,
Through many a danger and escape,
The tall ships passed the stormy cape;
For thee in foreign lands remote,
Beneath a burning, tropic clime,
The Indian peasant, chasing the wild goat,
Himself as swift and wild,
In falling, clutched the frail arbute,
The fibres of whose shallow root,
Uplifted from the soil, betrayed
The silver veins beneath it laid,
The buried treasures of the miser, Time.

But, lo! thy door is left ajar!
Thou hearest footsteps from afar!
And, at the sound,
Thou turnest round
With quick and questioning eyes,
Like one, who, in a foreign land,
Beholds on every hand
Some source of wonder and surprise!
And, restlessly, impatiently,
Thou strivest, strugglest, to be free,
The four walls of thy nursery
Are now like prison walls to thee.
No more thy mother's smiles,
No more the painted tiles,
Delight thee, nor the playthings on the floor,
That won thy little, beating heart before;
Thou strugglest for the open door.

Through these once solitary halls

Thy pattering footstep falls.
The sound of thy merry voice
Makes the old walls
Jubilant, and they rejoice
With the joy of thy young heart,
O'er the light of whose gladness
No shadows of sadness
From the sombre background of memory start.

Once, ah, once, within these walls,
One whom memory oft recalls,
The Father of his Country, dwelt.
And yonder meadows broad and damp
The fires of the besieging camp
Encircled with a burning belt.
Up and down these echoing stairs,
Heavy with the weight of cares,
Sounded his majestic tread;
Yes, within this very room
Sat he in those hours of gloom,
Weary both in heart and head.

But what are these grave thoughts to thee?
Out, out! into the open air!
Thy only dream is liberty,
Thou carest little how or where.
I see thee eager at thy play,
Now shouting to the apples on the tree,
With cheeks as round and red as they;
And now among the yellow stalks,
Among the flowering shrubs and plants,
As restless as the bee.
Along the garden walks,
The tracks of thy small carriage-wheels I trace;
And see at every turn how they efface
Whole villages of sand-roofed tents,
That rise like golden domes
Above the cavernous and secret homes
Of wandering and nomadic tribes of ants.
Ah, cruel little Tamerlane,
Who, with thy dreadful reign,
Dost persecute and overwhelm
These hapless Troglodytes of thy realm!
What! tired already! with those suppliant looks,
And voice more beautiful than a poet's books,
Or murmuring sound of water as it flows.
Thou comest back to parley with repose;
This rustic seat in the old apple-tree,

With its o'erhanging golden canopy
Of leaves illuminate with autumnal hues,
And shining with the argent light of dews,
Shall for a season be our place of rest.
Beneath us, like an oriole's pendent nest,
From which the laughing birds have taken wing,
By thee abandoned, hangs thy vacant swing.
Dream-like the waters of the river gleam;
A sailless vessel drops adown the stream,
And like it, to a sea as wide and deep,
Thou driftest gently down the tides of sleep.

O child! O new-born denizen
Of life's great city! on thy head
The glory of the morn is shed,
Like a celestial benison!
Here at the portal thou dost stand,
And with thy little hand
Thou openest the mysterious gate
Into the future's undiscovered land.
I see its valves expand,
As at the touch of Fate!
Into those realms of love and hate,
Into that darkness blank and drear,
By some prophetic feeling taught,
I launch the bold, adventurous thought,
Freighted with hope and fear;
As upon subterranean streams,
In caverns unexplored and dark,
Men sometimes launch a fragile bark,
Laden with flickering fire,
And watch its swift-receding beams,
Until at length they disappear,
And in the distant dark expire.

By what astrology of fear or hope
Dare I to cast thy horoscope!
Like the new moon thy life appears;
A little strip of silver light,
And widening outward into night
The shadowy disk of future years;
And yet upon its outer rim,
A luminous circle, faint and dim,
And scarcely visible to us here,
Rounds and completes the perfect sphere;
A prophecy and intimation,
A pale and feeble adumbration,
Of the great world of light, that lies

Behind all human destinies.

Ah! if thy fate, with anguish fraught,
Should be to wet the dusty soil
With the hot tears and sweat of toil,—
To struggle with imperious thought,
Until the overburdened brain,
Weary with labor, faint with pain,
Like a jarred pendulum, retain
Only its motion, not its power,—
Remember, in that perilous hour,
When most afflicted and oppressed,
From labor there shall come forth rest.

And if a more auspicious fate
On thy advancing steps await
Still let it ever be thy pride
To linger by the laborer's side;
With words of sympathy or song
To cheer the dreary march along
Of the great army of the poor,
O'er desert sand, o'er dangerous moor.
Nor to thyself the task shall be
Without reward; for thou shalt learn
The wisdom early to discern
True beauty in utility;
As great Pythagoras of yore,
Standing beside the blacksmith's door,
And hearing the hammers, as they smote
The anvils with a different note,
Stole from the varying tones, that hung
Vibrant on every iron tongue,
The secret of the sounding wire.
And formed the seven-chorded lyre.

Enough! I will not play the Seer;
I will no longer strive to ope
The mystic volume, where appear
The herald Hope, forerunning Fear,
And Fear, the pursuivant of Hope.
Thy destiny remains untold;
For, like Acestes' shaft of old,
The swift thought kindles as it flies,
And burns to ashes in the skies.

THE OCCULTATION OF ORION

I saw, as in a dream sublime,
The balance in the hand of Time.
O'er East and West its beam impended;
And day, with all its hours of light,
Was slowly sinking out of sight,
While, opposite, the scale of night
Silently with the stars ascended.

Like the astrologers of eld,
In that bright vision I beheld
Greater and deeper mysteries.
I saw, with its celestial keys,
Its chords of air, its frets of fire,
The Samian's great Aeolian lyre,
Rising through all its sevenfold bars,
From earth unto the fixed stars.
And through the dewy atmosphere,
Not only could I see, but hear,
Its wondrous and harmonious strings,
In sweet vibration, sphere by sphere,
From Dian's circle light and near,
Onward to vaster and wider rings.
Where, chanting through his beard of snows,
Majestic, mournful, Saturn goes,
And down the sunless realms of space
Reverberates the thunder of his bass.

Beneath the sky's triumphal arch
This music sounded like a march,
And with its chorus seemed to be
Preluding some great tragedy.
Sirius was rising in the east;
And, slow ascending one by one,
The kindling constellations shone.
Begirt with many a blazing star,
Stood the great giant Algebar,
Orion, hunter of the beast!
His sword hung gleaming by his side,
And, on his arm, the lion's hide
Scattered across the midnight air
The golden radiance of its hair.

The moon was pallid, but not faint;
And beautiful as some fair saint,
Serenely moving on her way
In hours of trial and dismay.
As if she heard the voice of God,

Unharmed with naked feet she trod
Upon the hot and burning stars,
As on the glowing coals and bars,
That were to prove her strength, and try
Her holiness and her purity.

Thus moving on, with silent pace,
And triumph in her sweet, pale face,
She reached the station of Orion.
Aghast he stood in strange alarm!
And suddenly from his outstretched arm
Down fell the red skin of the lion
Into the river at his feet.
His mighty club no longer beat
The forehead of the bull; but he
Reeled as of yore beside the sea,
When, blinded by Oenopion,
He sought the blacksmith at his forge,
And, climbing up the mountain gorge,
Fixed his blank eyes upon the sun.

Then, through the silence overhead,
An angel with a trumpet said,
"Forevermore, forevermore,
The reign of violence is o'er!"
And, like an instrument that flings
Its music on another's strings,
The trumpet of the angel cast
Upon the heavenly lyre its blast,
And on from sphere to sphere the words
Re-echoed down the burning chords,—
"Forevermore, forevermore,
The reign of violence is o'er!"

THE BRIDGE

I stood on the bridge at midnight,
As the clocks were striking the hour,
And the moon rose o'er the city,
Behind the dark church-tower.

I saw her bright reflection
In the waters under me,
Like a golden goblet falling
And sinking into the sea.

And far in the hazy distance
Of that lovely night in June,
The blaze of the flaming furnace
Gleamed redder than the moon.

Among the long, black rafters
The wavering shadows lay,
And the current that came from the ocean
Seemed to lift and bear them away;

As, sweeping and eddying through them,
Rose the belated tide,
And, streaming into the moonlight,
The seaweed floated wide.

And like those waters rushing
Among the wooden piers,
A flood of thoughts came o'er me
That filled my eyes with tears.

How often, oh, how often,
In the days that had gone by,
I had stood on that bridge at midnight
And gazed on that wave and sky!

How often, oh, how often,
I had wished that the ebbing tide
Would bear me away on its bosom
O'er the ocean wild and wide!

For my heart was hot and restless,
And my life was full of care,
And the burden laid upon me
Seemed greater than I could bear.

But now it has fallen from me,
It is buried in the sea;
And only the sorrow of others
Throws its shadow over me.

Yet whenever I cross the river
On its bridge with wooden piers,
Like the odor of brine from the ocean
Comes the thought of other years.

And I think how many thousands
Of care-encumbered men,
Each bearing his burden of sorrow,

Have crossed the bridge since then.

I see the long procession
Still passing to and fro,
The young heart hot and restless,
And the old subdued and slow!

And forever and forever,
As long as the river flows,
As long as the heart has passions,
As long as life has woes;

The moon and its broken reflection
And its shadows shall appear,
As the symbol of love in heaven,
And its wavering image here.

TO THE DRIVING CLOUD

Gloomy and dark art thou, O chief of the mighty Omahas;
Gloomy and dark as the driving cloud, whose name thou hast taken!
Wrapt in thy scarlet blanket, I see thee stalk through the city's
Narrow and populous streets, as once by the margin of rivers
Stalked those birds unknown, that have left us only their footprints.
What, in a few short years, will remain of thy race but the footprints?

How canst thou walk these streets, who hast trod the green turf of the prairies!
How canst thou breathe this air, who hast breathed the sweet air of the mountains!
Ah! 't is in vain that with lordly looks of disdain thou dost challenge
Looks of disdain in return, and question these walls and these pavements,
Claiming the soil for thy hunting-grounds, while down-trodden millions
Starve in the garrets of Europe, and cry from its caverns that they, too,
Have been created heirs of the earth, and claim its division!

Back, then, back to thy woods in the regions west of the Wabash!
There as a monarch thou reignest. In autumn the leaves of the maple
Pave the floors of thy palace-halls with gold, and in summer
Pine-trees waft through its chambers the odorous breath of their branches.
There thou art strong and great, a hero, a tamer of horses!
There thou chasest the stately stag on the banks of the Elkhorn,
Or by the roar of the Running-Water, or where the Omaha
Calls thee, and leaps through the wild ravine like a brave of the Blackfeet!

Hark! what murmurs arise from the heart of those mountainous deserts?
Is it the cry of the Foxes and Crows, or the mighty Behemoth,
Who, unharmed, on his tusks once caught the bolts of the thunder,

And now lurks in his lair to destroy the race of the red man?
Far more fatal to thee and thy race than the Crows and the Foxes,
Far more fatal to thee and thy race than the tread of Behemoth,
Lo! the big thunder-canoe, that steadily breasts the Missouri's
Merciless current! and yonder, afar on the prairies, the camp-fires
Gleam through the night; and the cloud of dust in the gray of the daybreak
Marks not the buffalo's track, nor the Mandan's dexterous horse-race;
It is a caravan, whitening the desert where dwell the Camanches!
Ha! how the breath of these Saxons and Celts, like the blast of the east-wind,
Drifts evermore to the west the scanty smokes of thy wigwams!

SONGS

THE DAY IS DONE

The day is done, and the darkness
Falls from the wings of Night,
As a feather is wafted downward
From an eagle in his flight.

I see the lights of the village
Gleam through the rain and the mist,
And a feeling of sadness comes o'er me
That my soul cannot resist:

A feeling of sadness and longing,
That is not akin to pain,
And resembles sorrow only
As the mist resembles the rain.

Come, read to me some poem,
Some simple and heartfelt lay,
That shall soothe this restless feeling,
And banish the thoughts of day.

Not from the grand old masters,
Not from the bards sublime,
Whose distant footsteps echo
Through the corridors of Time.

For, like strains of martial music,
Their mighty thoughts suggest
Life's endless toil and endeavor;
And to-night I long for rest.

Read from some humbler poet,

Whose songs gushed from his heart,
As showers from the clouds of summer,
Or tears from the eyelids start;

Who, through long days of labor,
And nights devoid of ease,
Still heard in his soul the music
Of wonderful melodies.

Such songs have power to quiet
The restless pulse of care,
And come like the benediction
That follows after prayer.

Then read from the treasured volume
The poem of thy choice,
And lend to the rhyme of the poet
The beauty of thy voice.

And the night shall be filled with music
And the cares, that infest the day,
Shall fold their tents, like the Arabs,
And as silently steal away.

AFTERNOON IN FEBRUARY

The day is ending,
The night is descending;
The marsh is frozen,
The river dead.

Through clouds like ashes
The red sun flashes
On village windows
That glimmer red.

The snow recommences;
The buried fences
Mark no longer
The road o'er the plain;

While through the meadows,
Like fearful shadows,
Slowly passes
A funeral train.

The bell is pealing,
And every feeling
Within me responds
To the dismal knell;

Shadows are trailing,
My heart is bewailing
And tolling within
Like a funeral bell.

TO AN OLD DANISH SONG-BOOK

Welcome, my old friend,
Welcome to a foreign fireside,
While the sullen gales of autumn
Shake the windows.

The ungrateful world
Has, it seems, dealt harshly with thee,
Since, beneath the skies of Denmark,
First I met thee.

There are marks of age,
There are thumb-marks on thy margin,
Made by hands that clasped thee rudely,
At the alehouse.

Soiled and dull thou art;
Yellow are thy time-worn pages,
As the russet, rain-molested
Leaves of autumn.

Thou art stained with wine
Scattered from hilarious goblets,
As the leaves with the libations
Of Olympus.

Yet dost thou recall
Days departed, half-forgotten,
When in dreamy youth I wandered
By the Baltic,—

When I paused to hear
The old ballad of King Christian
Shouted from suburban taverns
In the twilight.

Thou recallest bards,
Who in solitary chambers,
And with hearts by passion wasted,
Wrote thy pages.

Thou recallest homes
Where thy songs of love and friendship
Made the gloomy Northern winter
Bright as summer.

Once some ancient Scald,
In his bleak, ancestral Iceland,
Chanted staves of these old ballads
To the Vikings.

Once in Elsinore,
At the court of old King Hamlet
Yorick and his boon companions
Sang these ditties.

Once Prince Frederick's Guard
Sang them in their smoky barracks;—
Suddenly the English cannon
Joined the chorus!

Peasants in the field,
Sailors on the roaring ocean,
Students, tradesmen, pale mechanics,
All have sung them.

Thou hast been their friend;
They, alas! have left thee friendless!
Yet at least by one warm fireside
Art thou welcome.

And, as swallows build
In these wide, old-fashioned chimneys,
So thy twittering songs shall nestle
In my bosom,—

Quiet, close, and warm,
Sheltered from all molestation,
And recalling by their voices
Youth and travel.

Vogelweid the Minnesinger,
When he left this world of ours,
Laid his body in the cloister,
Under Wurtzburg's minster towers.

And he gave the monks his treasures,
Gave them all with this behest:
They should feed the birds at noontide
Daily on his place of rest;

Saying, "From these wandering minstrels
I have learned the art of song;
Let me now repay the lessons
They have taught so well and long."

Thus the bard of love departed;
And, fulfilling his desire,
On his tomb the birds were feasted
By the children of the choir.

Day by day, o'er tower and turret,
In foul weather and in fair,
Day by day, in vaster numbers,
Flocked the poets of the air.

On the tree whose heavy branches
Overshadowed all the place,
On the pavement, on the tombstone,
On the poet's sculptured face,

On the cross-bars of each window,
On the lintel of each door,
They renewed the War of Wartburg,
Which the bard had fought before.

There they sang their merry carols,
Sang their lauds on every side;
And the name their voices uttered
Was the name of Vogelweid.

Till at length the portly abbot
Murmured, "Why this waste of food?
Be it changed to loaves henceforward
For our tasting brotherhood."

Then in vain o'er tower and turret,

From the walls and woodland nests,
When the minster bells rang noontide,
Gathered the unwelcome guests.

Then in vain, with cries discordant,
Clamorous round the Gothic spire,
Screamed the feathered Minnesingers
For the children of the choir.

Time has long effaced the inscriptions
On the cloister's funeral stones,
And tradition only tells us
Where repose the poet's bones.

But around the vast cathedral,
By sweet echoes multiplied,
Still the birds repeat the legend,
And the name of Vogelweid.

DRINKING SONG

INSCRIPTION FOR AN ANTIQUE PITCHER

Come, old friend! sit down and listen!
From the pitcher, placed between us,
How the waters laugh and glisten
In the head of old Silenus!

Old Silenus, bloated, drunken,
Led by his inebriate Satyrs;
On his breast his head is sunken,
Vacantly he leers and chatters.

Fauns with youthful Bacchus follow;
Ivy crowns that brow supernal
As the forehead of Apollo,
And possessing youth eternal.

Round about him, fair Bacchantes,
Bearing cymbals, flutes, and thyrses,
Wild from Naxian groves, or Zante's
Vineyards, sing delirious verses.

Thus he won, through all the nations,
Bloodless victories, and the farmer
Bore, as trophies and oblations,

Vines for banners, ploughs for armor.

Judged by no o'erzealous rigor,
Much this mystic throng expresses:
Bacchus was the type of vigor,
And Silenus of excesses.

These are ancient ethnic revels,
Of a faith long since forsaken;
Now the Satyrs, changed to devils,
Frighten mortals wine-o'ertaken.

Now to rivulets from the mountains
Point the rods of fortune-tellers;
Youth perpetual dwells in fountains,—
Not in flasks, and casks, and cellars.

Claudius, though he sang of flagons
And huge tankards filled with Rhenish,
From that fiery blood of dragons
Never would his own replenish.

Even Redi, though he chaunted
Bacchus in the Tuscan valleys,
Never drank the wine he vaunted
In his dithyrambic sallies.

Then with water fill the pitcher
Wreathed about with classic fables;
Ne'er Falernian threw a richer
Light upon Lucullus' tables.

Come, old friend, sit down and listen
As it passes thus between us,
How its wavelets laugh and glisten
In the head of old Silenus!

THE OLD CLOCK ON THE STAIRS

*L'eternite est une pendule, dont le balancier dit et redit sans cesse ces deux mots seulement dans le silence des tombeaux: "Toujours! jamais! Jamais! toujours!"—**JACQUES BRIDAINE**.*

Somewhat back from the village street
Stands the old-fashioned country-seat.
Across its antique portico
Tall poplar-trees their shadows throw;

And from its station in the hall
An ancient timepiece says to all,—
"Forever—never!
Never—forever!"

Half-way up the stairs it stands,
And points and beckons with its hands
From its case of massive oak,
Like a monk, who, under his cloak,
Crosses himself, and sighs, alas!
With sorrowful voice to all who pass,—
"Forever—never!
Never—forever!"

By day its voice is low and light;
But in the silent dead of night,
Distinct as a passing footstep's fall,
It echoes along the vacant hall,
Along the ceiling, along the floor,
And seems to say, at each chamber-door,—
"Forever—never!
Never—forever!"

Through days of sorrow and of mirth,
Through days of death and days of birth,
Through every swift vicissitude
Of changeful time, unchanged it has stood,
And as if, like God, it all things saw,
It calmly repeats those words of awe,—
"Forever—never!
Never—forever!"

In that mansion used to be
Free-hearted Hospitality;
His great fires up the chimney roared;
The stranger feasted at his board;
But, like the skeleton at the feast,
That warning timepiece never ceased,—
"Forever—never!
Never—forever!"

There groups of merry children played,
There youths and maidens dreaming strayed;
O precious hours! O golden prime,
And affluence of love and time!
Even as a Miser counts his gold,
Those hours the ancient timepiece told,—
"Forever—never!

Never—forever!"

From that chamber, clothed in white,
The bride came forth on her wedding night;
There, in that silent room below,
The dead lay in his shroud of snow;
And in the hush that followed the prayer,
Was heard the old clock on the stair,—
"Forever—never!
Never—forever!"

All are scattered now and fled,
Some are married, some are dead;
And when I ask, with throbs of pain.
"Ah! when shall they all meet again?"
As in the days long since gone by,
The ancient timepiece makes reply,—
"Forever—never!
Never—forever!"

Never here, forever there,
Where all parting, pain, and care,
And death, and time shall disappear,—
Forever there, but never here!
The horologe of Eternity
Sayeth this incessantly,—
"Forever—never!
Never—forever!"

THE ARROW AND THE SONG

I shot an arrow into the air,
It fell to earth, I knew not where;
For, so swiftly it flew, the sight
Could not follow it in its flight.

I breathed a song into the air,
It fell to earth, I knew not where;
For who has sight so keen and strong,
That it can follow the flight of song?

Long, long afterward, in an oak
I found the arrow, still unbroke;
And the song, from beginning to end,
I found again in the heart of a friend.

SONNETS

MEZZO CAMMIN

Half of my life is gone, and I have let
The years slip from me and have not fulfilled
The aspiration of my youth, to build
Some tower of song with lofty parapet.
Not indolence, nor pleasure, nor the fret
Of restless passions chat would not be stilled,
But sorrow, and a care that almost killed,
Kept me from what I may accomplish yet;
Though, half way up the hill, I see the Past
Lying beneath me with its sounds and sights,—
A city in the twilight dim and vast,
With smoking roofs, soft bells, and gleaming lights.—
And hear above me on the autumnal blast
The cataract of Death far thundering from the heights.

THE EVENING STAR

Lo! in the painted oriel of the West,
Whose panes the sunken sun incarnadines,
Like a fair lady at her casement, shines
The evening star, the star of love and rest!
And then anon she doth herself divest
Of all her radiant garments, and reclines
Behind the sombre screen of yonder pines,
With slumber and soft dreams of love oppressed.
O my beloved, my sweet Hesperus!
My morning and my evening star of love!
My best and gentlest lady! even thus,
As that fair planet in the sky above,
Dost thou retire unto thy rest at night,
And from thy darkened window fades the light.

AUTUMN

Thou comest, Autumn, heralded by the rain,
With banners, by great gales incessant fanned,
Brighter than brightest silks of Samarcand,
And stately oxen harnessed to thy wain!

Thou standest, like imperial Charlemagne,
Upon thy bridge of gold; thy royal hand
Outstretched with benedictions o'er the land,
Blessing the farms through all thy vast domain!
Thy shield is the red harvest moon, suspended
So long beneath the heaven's o'er-hanging eaves;
Thy steps are by the farmer's prayers attended;
Like flames upon an altar shine the sheaves;
And, following thee, in thy ovation splendid,
Thine almoner, the wind, scatters the golden leaves!

DANTE

Tuscan, that wanderest through the realms of gloom,
With thoughtful pace, and sad, majestic eyes,
Stern thoughts and awful from thy soul arise,
Like Farinata from his fiery tomb.
Thy sacred song is like the trump of doom;
Yet in thy heart what human sympathies,
What soft compassion glows, as in the skies
The tender stars their clouded lamps relume!
Methinks I see thee stand, with pallid cheeks,
By Fra Hilario in his diocese,
As up the convent-walls, in golden streaks,
The ascending sunbeams mark the day's decrease;
And, as he asks what there the stranger seeks,
Thy voice along the cloister whispers, "Peace!"

CURFEW

I.

Solemnly, mournfully,
Dealing its dole,
The Curfew Bell
Is beginning to toll.

Cover the embers,
And put out the light;
Toil comes with the morning,
And rest with the night.

Dark grow the windows,
And quenched is the fire;

Sound fades into silence,—
All footsteps retire.

No voice in the chambers,
No sound in the hall!
Sleep and oblivion
Reign over all!

II.

The book is completed,
And closed, like the day;
And the hand that has written it
Lays it away.

Dim grow its fancies;
Forgotten they lie;
Like coals in the ashes,
They darken and die.

Song sinks into silence,
The story is told,
The windows are darkened,
The hearth-stone is cold.

Darker and darker
The black shadows fall;
Sleep and oblivion
Reign over all.

KERAMOS

Turn, turn, my wheel? Turn round and round
Without a pause, without a sound:
So spins the flying world away!
This clay, well mixed with marl and sand,
Follows the motion of my hand;
Far some must follow, and some command,
Though all are made of clay!

Thus sang the Potter at his task
Beneath the blossoming hawthorn-tree,
While o'er his features, like a mask,
The quilted sunshine and leaf-shade
Moved, as the boughs above him swayed,

And clothed him, till he seemed to be
A figure woven in tapestry,
So sumptuously was he arrayed
In that magnificent attire
Of sable tissue flaked with fire.
Like a magician he appeared,
A conjurer without book or beard;
And while he plied his magic art—
For it was magical to me—
I stood in silence and apart,
And wondered more and more to see
That shapeless, lifeless mass of clay
Rise up to meet the master's hand,
And now contract and now expand,
And even his slightest touch obey;
While ever in a thoughtful mood
He sang his ditty, and at times
Whistled a tune between the rhymes,
As a melodious interlude.

Turn, turn, my wheel! All things must change
To something new, to something strange;
Nothing that is can pause or stay;
The moon will wax, the moon will wane,
The mist and cloud will turn to rain,
The rain to mist and cloud again,
To-morrow be to-day.

Thus still the Potter sang, and still,
By some unconscious act of will,
The melody and even the words
Were intermingled with my thought
As bits of colored thread are caught
And woven into nests of birds.
And thus to regions far remote,
Beyond the ocean's vast expanse,
This wizard in the motley coat
Transported me on wings of song,
And by the northern shores of France
Bore me with restless speed along.
What land is this that seems to be
A mingling of the land and sea?
This land of sluices, dikes, and dunes?
This water-net, that tessellates
The landscape? this unending maze
Of gardens, through whose latticed gates
The imprisoned pinks and tulips gaze;
Where in long summer afternoons

The sunshine, softened by the haze,
Comes streaming down as through a screen;
Where over fields and pastures green
The painted ships float high in air,
And over all and everywhere
The sails of windmills sink and soar
Like wings of sea-gulls on the shore?

What land is this? Yon pretty town
Is Delft, with all its wares displayed;
The pride, the market-place, the crown
And centre of the Potter's trade.
See! every house and room is bright
With glimmers of reflected light
From plates that on the dresser shine;
Flagons to foam with Flemish beer,
Or sparkle with the Rhenish wine,
And pilgrim flasks with fleurs-de-lis,
And ships upon a rolling sea,
And tankards pewter topped, and queer
With comic mask and musketeer!
Each hospitable chimney smiles
A welcome from its painted tiles;
The parlor walls, the chamber floors,
The stairways and the corridors,
The borders of the garden walks,
Are beautiful with fadeless flowers,
That never droop in winds or showers,
And never wither on their stalks.

Turn, turn, my wheel! All life is brief;
What now is bud wilt soon be leaf,
What now is leaf will soon decay;
The wind blows east, the wind blows west;
The blue eyes in the robin's nest
Will soon have wings and beak and breast,
And flutter and fly away.

Now southward through the air I glide,
The song my only pursuivant,
And see across the landscape wide
The blue Charente, upon whose tide
The belfries and the spires of Saintes
Ripple and rock from side to side,
As, when an earthquake rends its walls,
A crumbling city reels and falls.

Who is it in the suburbs here,

This Potter, working with such cheer,
In this mean house, this mean attire,
His manly features bronzed with fire,
Whose figulines and rustic wares
Scarce find him bread from day to day?
This madman, as the people say,
Who breaks his tables and his chairs
To feed his furnace fires, nor cares
Who goes unfed if they are fed,
Nor who may live if they are dead?
This alchemist with hollow cheeks
And sunken, searching eyes, who seeks,
By mingled earths and ores combined
With potency of fire, to find
Some new enamel, hard and bright,
His dream, his passion, his delight?

O Palissy! within thy breast
Burned the hot fever of unrest;
Thine was the prophets vision, thine
The exultation, the divine
Insanity of noble minds,
That never falters nor abates,
But labors and endures and waits,
Till all that it foresees it finds,
Or what it cannot find creates!

Turn, turn, my wheel! This earthen jar
A touch can make, a touch can mar;
And shall it to the Potter say,
What makest thou. Thou hast no hand?
As men who think to understand
A world by their Creator planned,
Who wiser is than they.

Still guided by the dreamy song,
As in a trance I float along
Above the Pyrenean chain,
Above the fields and farms of Spain,
Above the bright Majorcan isle,
That lends its softened name to art,—
A spot, a dot upon the chart,
Whose little towns, red-roofed with tile,
Are ruby-lustred with the light
Of blazing furnaces by night,
And crowned by day with wreaths of smoke.
Then eastward, wafted in my flight
On my enchanter's magic cloak,

I sail across the Tyrrhene Sea
Into the land of Italy,
And o'er the windy Apennines,
Mantled and musical with pines.

The palaces, the princely halls,
The doors of houses and the walls
Of churches and of belfry towers,
Cloister and castle, street and mart,
Are garlanded and gay with flowers
That blossom in the fields of art.
Here Gubbio's workshops gleam and glow
With brilliant, iridescent dyes,
The dazzling whiteness of the snow,
The cobalt blue of summer skies;
And vase and scutcheon, cup and plate,
In perfect finish emulate
Faenza, Florence, Pesaro.

Forth from Urbino's gate there came
A youth with the angelic name
Of Raphael, in form and face
Himself angelic, and divine
In arts of color and design.
From him Francesco Xanto caught
Something of his transcendent grace,
And into fictile fabrics wrought
Suggestions of the master's thought.
Nor less Maestro Giorgio shines
With madre-perl and golden lines
Of arabesques, and interweaves
His birds and fruits and flowers and leaves
About some landscape, shaded brown,
With olive tints on rock and town.
Behold this cup within whose bowl,
Upon a ground of deepest blue
With yellow-lustred stars o'erlaid,
Colors of every tint and hue
Mingle in one harmonious whole!
With large blue eyes and steadfast gaze,
Her yellow hair in net and braid,
Necklace and ear-rings all ablaze
With golden lustre o'er the glaze,
A woman's portrait; on the scroll,
Cana, the Beautiful! A name
Forgotten save for such brief fame
As this memorial can bestow,—
A gift some lover long ago

Gave with his heart to this fair dame.

A nobler title to renown
Is thine, O pleasant Tuscan town,
Seated beside the Arno's stream;
For Lucca della Robbia there
Created forms so wondrous fair,
They made thy sovereignty supreme.
These choristers with lips of stone,
Whose music is not heard, but seen,
Still chant, as from their organ-screen,
Their Maker's praise; nor these alone,
But the more fragile forms of clay,
Hardly less beautiful than they,
These saints and angels that adorn
The walls of hospitals, and tell
The story of good deeds so well
That poverty seems less forlorn,
And life more like a holiday.

Here in this old neglected church,
That long eludes the traveller's search,
Lies the dead bishop on his tomb;
Earth upon earth he slumbering lies,
Life-like and death-like in the gloom;
Garlands of fruit and flowers in bloom
And foliage deck his resting place;
A shadow in the sightless eyes,
A pallor on the patient face,
Made perfect by the furnace heat;
All earthly passions and desires
Burnt out by purgatorial fires;
Seeming to say, "Our years are fleet,
And to the weary death is sweet."

But the most wonderful of all
The ornaments on tomb or wall
That grace the fair Ausonian shores
Are those the faithful earth restores,
Near some Apulian town concealed,
In vineyard or in harvest field,—
Vases and urns and bas-reliefs,
Memorials of forgotten griefs,
Or records of heroic deeds
Of demigods and mighty chiefs:
Figures that almost move and speak,
And, buried amid mould and weeds,
Still in their attitudes attest

The presence of the graceful Greek,—
Achilles in his armor dressed,
Alcides with the Cretan bull,
And Aphrodite with her boy,
Or lovely Helena of Troy,
Still living and still beautiful.

Turn, turn, my wheel! 'T is nature's plan
The child should grow into the man,
The man grow wrinkled, old, and gray;
In youth the heart exults and sings,
The pulses leap, the feet have wings;
In age the cricket chirps, and brings
The harvest home of day.

And now the winds that southward blow,
And cool the hot Sicilian isle,
Bear me away. I see below
The long line of the Libyan Nile,
Flooding and feeding the parched land
With annual ebb and overflow,
A fallen palm whose branches lie
Beneath the Abyssinian sky,
Whose roots are in Egyptian sands,
On either bank huge water-wheels,
Belted with jars and dripping weeds,
Send forth their melancholy moans,
As if, in their gray mantles hid,
Dead anchorites of the Thebaid
Knelt on the shore and told their beads,
Beating their breasts with loud appeals
And penitential tears and groans.

This city, walled and thickly set
With glittering mosque and minaret,
Is Cairo, in whose gay bazaars
The dreaming traveller first inhales
The perfume of Arabian gales,
And sees the fabulous earthen jars,
Huge as were those wherein the maid
Morgiana found the Forty Thieves
Concealed in midnight ambuscade;
And seeing, more than half believes
The fascinating tales that run
Through all the Thousand Nights and One,
Told by the fair Scheherezade.

More strange and wonderful than these

Are the Egyptian deities,
Ammonn, and Emeth, and the grand
Osiris, holding in his hand
The lotus; Isis, crowned and veiled;
The sacred Ibis, and the Sphinx;
Bracelets with blue enamelled links;
The Scarabee in emerald mailed,
Or spreading wide his funeral wings;
Lamps that perchance their night-watch kept
O'er Cleopatra while she slept,—
All plundered from the tombs of kings.

Turn, turn, my wheel! The human race,
Of every tongue, of every place,
Caucasian, Coptic, or Malay,
All that inhabit this great earth,
Whatever be their rank or worth,
Are kindred and allied by birth,
And made of the same clay.

O'er desert sands, o'er gulf and bay,
O'er Ganges and o'er Himalay,
Bird-like I fly, and flying sing,
To flowery kingdoms of Cathay,
And bird-like poise on balanced wing
Above the town of King-te-tching,
A burning town, or seeming so,—
Three thousand furnaces that glow
Incessantly, and fill the air
With smoke uprising, gyre on gyre
And painted by the lurid glare,
Of jets and flashes of red fire.

As leaves that in the autumn fall,
Spotted and veined with various hues,
Are swept along the avenues,
And lie in heaps by hedge and wall,
So from this grove of chimneys whirled
To all the markets of the world,
These porcelain leaves are wafted on,—
Light yellow leaves with spots and stains
Of violet and of crimson dye,
Or tender azure of a sky
Just washed by gentle April rains,
And beautiful with celadon.

Nor less the coarser household wares,—
The willow pattern, that we knew

In childhood, with its bridge of blue
Leading to unknown thoroughfares;
The solitary man who stares
At the white river flowing through
Its arches, the fantastic trees
And wild perspective of the view;
And intermingled among these
The tiles that in our nurseries
Filled us with wonder and delight,
Or haunted us in dreams at night.

And yonder by Nankin, behold!
The Tower of Porcelain, strange and old,
Uplifting to the astonished skies
Its ninefold painted balconies,
With balustrades of twining leaves,
And roofs of tile, beneath whose eaves
Hang porcelain bells that all the time
Ring with a soft, melodious chime;
While the whole fabric is ablaze
With varied tints, all fused in one
Great mass of color, like a maze
Of flowers illumined by the sun.

Turn, turn, my wheel! What is begun
At daybreak must at dark be done,
To-morrow will be another day;
To-morrow the hot furnace flame
Will search the heart and try the frame,
And stamp with honor or with shame
These vessels made of clay.

Cradled and rocked in Eastern seas,
The islands of the Japanese
Beneath me lie; o'er lake and plain
The stork, the heron, and the crane
Through the clear realms of azure drift,
And on the hillside I can see
The villages of Imari,
Whose thronged and flaming workshops lift
Their twisted columns of smoke on high,
Cloud cloisters that in ruins lie,
With sunshine streaming through each rift,
And broken arches of blue sky.

All the bright flowers that fill the land,
Ripple of waves on rock or sand,
The snow on Fusiyama's cone,

The midnight heaven so thickly sown
With constellations of bright stars,
The leaves that rustle, the reeds that make
A whisper by each stream and lake,
The saffron dawn, the sunset red,
Are painted on these lovely jars;
Again the skylark sings, again
The stork, the heron, and the crane
Float through the azure overhead,
The counterfeit and counterpart
Of Nature reproduced in Art.

Art is the child of Nature; yes,
Her darling child, in whom we trace
The features of the mother's face,
Her aspect and her attitude,
All her majestic loveliness
Chastened and softened and subdued
Into a more attractive grace,
And with a human sense imbued.
He is the greatest artist, then,
Whether of pencil or of pen,
Who follows Nature. Never man,
As artist or as artisan,
Pursuing his own fantasies,
Can touch the human heart, or please,
Or satisfy our nobler needs,
As he who sets his willing feet
In Nature's footprints, light and fleet,
And follows fearless where she leads.

Thus mused I on that morn in May,
Wrapped in my visions like the Seer,
Whose eyes behold not what is near,
But only what is far away,
When, suddenly sounding peal on peal,
The church-bell from the neighboring town
Proclaimed the welcome hour of noon.
The Potter heard, and stopped his wheel,
His apron on the grass threw down,
Whistled his quiet little tune,
Not overloud nor overlong,
And ended thus his simple song:

Stop, stop, my wheel! Too soon, too soon
The noon will be the afternoon,
Too soon to-day be yesterday;
Behind us in our path we cast

The broken potsherds of the past,
And all are ground to dust a last,
And trodden into clay!

Henry Wadsworth Longfellow was born on February 27th, 1807 in Portland, Maine (then part of Massachusetts) to Stephen Longfellow and Zilpah (nee Wadsworth) Longfellow. His father was a lawyer, and his maternal grandfather, Peleg Wadsworth, was a general in the American Revolutionary War and a Member of Congress.

It was a large family. Longfellow was the second of eight children; his siblings were Stephen (1805), Elizabeth (1808), Anne (1810), Alexander (1814), Mary (1816), Ellen (1818) and Samuel (1819).

Longfellow attended a dame school at the age of three and by age six was enrolled at the private Portland Academy. He was very studious and quickly became fluent in Latin. His mother encouraged his love of reading and learning and introduced him to many literary classics.

He published his first poem, a patriotic four-stanza affair entitled "The Battle of Lovell's Pond", in the Portland Gazette on November 17, 1820. He remained at the Portland Academy until he was fourteen. As a child, he spent much of his summers at his grandfather Peleg's farm in the nearby town of Hiram.

In the fall of 1822, the 15-year-old Longfellow enrolled at Bowdoin College in Brunswick, Maine. His grandfather was a founder of the college and his father a trustee. Here he met and befriended Nathaniel Hawthorne. Longfellow was already thinking of a career in literature. In his senior year he wrote to his father: "I will not disguise it in the least... the fact is, I most eagerly aspire after future eminence in literature, my whole soul burns most ardently after it, and every earthly thought centers in it... I am almost confident in believing, that if I can ever rise in the world it must be by the exercise of my talents in the wide field of literature."

Poetry was the writing form he felt most at ease with and he offered poems to many newspapers and magazines. Between January 1824 and graduation in 1825, he had almost 40 poems published, over half of which were in the short-lived Boston periodical The United States Literary Gazette.

When Longfellow graduated, he was ranked a pleasing fourth in the class, and had been elected to Phi Beta Kappa. He was quickly offered the post of professor of modern languages at his alma mater.

Accounts suggest that part of the requirement of acceptance was to tour Europe to become more immersed in both languages and cultures. Longfellow began his tour of Europe in May 1826 aboard the ship Cadmus. His travels in Europe would last three years and cost his father the princely sum of $2,604.24. He visited France, Spain, Italy, Germany and England before returning to the United States in mid-August 1829.

His stock of languages now included French, Spanish, Portuguese, and German, and impressively, mostly without any formal instruction.

On August 27th, 1829, he wrote to the president of Bowdoin that he was turning down the professorship because he considered the $600 salary "disproportionate to the duties required". The trustees countered by raising the salary to $800 and an additional $100 to serve as the college's librarian, a post which required only one hour's attention a day.

On September 14th, 1831, Longfellow married Mary Storer Potter, a childhood friend from Portland. The couple settled in Brunswick. Longfellow now published several non-fiction and fiction prose pieces inspired by his friend Washington Irving, whom he had met in Madrid during his travels, these included "The Indian Summer" and "The Bald Eagle" in 1833.

During his years teaching at the college, he translated textbooks in French, Italian and Spanish; his first published book was in 1833, a translation of the poetry of the medieval Spanish poet Jorge Manrique. A travel book, Outre-Mer: A Pilgrimage Beyond the Sea, was first published in serial form before a book edition in 1835.

In December 1834, Longfellow received a letter from Josiah Quincy III, president of Harvard College, offering him the Smith Professorship of Modern Languages with the condition that he first spend a year or so abroad. The Longfellow's set off for Europe. He would now be able to add German, Dutch, Danish, Swedish, Finnish, and Icelandic to his repertoire of languages.

During the trip they discovered that Mary was pregnant. Sadly, in October 1835, she miscarried some six months into the pregnancy. Then followed several weeks of illness and at the age of 22 on November 29th, 1835 she died. Longfellow had her body embalmed, placed in a lead coffin itself inside an oak coffin which was then shipped to Mount Auburn Cemetery near Boston. He wrote movingly "One thought occupies me night and day... She is dead—She is dead! All day I am weary and sad".

Back in the United States, Longfellow took up the professorship at Harvard. He was required to live in Cambridge, close to the campus and rented rooms at the Craigie House in the spring of 1837. The home, built in 1759, had once been the headquarters of George Washington during the Siege of Boston.

Longfellow now felt able to publish again, starting with the collection Voices of the Night in 1839. It was mainly comprised of translations together with nine original poems and seven poems written back in his teenage years.

His romantic interests also began to surface again. He had begun to court Frances 'Fanny' Appleton, daughter of the Boston industrialist Nathan Appleton. At first, the independent-minded Appleton was not interested in marriage but Longfellow was determined. In July 1839, he wrote to a friend: "Victory hangs doubtful. The lady says she will not! I say she shall! It is not pride, but the madness of passion".

In late 1839, Longfellow published Hyperion, a book in prose inspired by his trips abroad and his still unsuccessful courtship of Fanny Appleton. Amidst this, Longfellow fell into "periods of neurotic depression with moments of panic" and required a six-month leave of absence from Harvard to attend a health spa in the former Marienberg Benedictine Convent at Boppard in Germany.

Ballads and Other Poems was published in 1841 and included "The Village Blacksmith" and "The Wreck of the Hesperus". His reputation as a poet, and a commercial one at that, was set.

Longfellow published a play in 1842, The Spanish Student, based on his memories from his time in Spain in the 1820s. A small collection, Poems on Slavery, was also published in 1842. This was Longfellow's first public support of abolitionism. However, as Longfellow himself said, the poems were "so mild that even a Slaveholder might read them without losing his appetite for breakfast". The New England Anti-Slavery Association, however, was satisfied enough with the intent of the collection to reprint it for their own distribution.

On May 10th, 1843, after seven years in pursuit, Longfellow received a letter from Fanny Appleton agreeing to marry him. He was elated and immediately walked 90 minutes to meet her at her house.

Nathan Appleton bought the Craigie House as a wedding present to the pair. Longfellow lived there for the rest of his life. His love for Fanny is evident from Longfellow's only love poem, the sonnet "The Evening Star", written in October 1845:

"O my beloved, my sweet Hesperus!
My morning and my evening star of love!"

He once attended a ball without her and said, "The lights seemed dimmer, the music sadder, the flowers fewer, and the women less fair."

Longfellow and Fanny had six children: Charles Appleton (1844), Ernest Wadsworth (1845), Fanny (1847, who died in infancy), Alice Mary (1850), Edith (1853), and Anne Allegra (1855).

Aware of his growing stature and his ability to influence others he also encouraged and supported many other translators. In 1845, he published The Poets and Poetry of Europe, a large 800-page compendium of translated works by other writers. Longfellow intended the anthology "to bring together, into a compact and convenient form, as large an amount as possible of those English translations which are scattered through many volumes, and are not accessible to the general reader".

On November 1st, 1847, the epic poem Evangeline was published.

Longfellow's literary income was now becoming quite substantial: in 1840, he had made $219 but by 1850 it had grown to a very promising $1,900.

On June 14th, 1853, Longfellow held a farewell dinner party at his Cambridge home for his great friend Nathaniel Hawthorne, who was preparing to move overseas.

In 1854, Longfellow retired from Harvard, devoting himself entirely to writing. He would be awarded an honorary doctorate of laws from Harvard in 1859.

The Song of Haiwatha, his epic poem, and perhaps his best known and enjoyed work was published in 1855.

On a hot July 9th day, 1861, Fanny was putting several locks of her children's hair into an envelope and making attempts to seal it with hot sealing wax while Longfellow took a nap. The circumstances of what happened next vary but the actuality is that Fanny's dress caught fire. Her screams awakened Longfellow who rushed to help her and threw a rug over her and stifled the flames with his own body as best he could, but Fanny was already horrifically burned.

A doctor was called and Fanny was taken to her room to recover. She was in and out of consciousness throughout the night and was also administered ether. The next morning, July 10th, 1861, she died shortly after 10 o'clock after asking for a cup of coffee.

Longfellow, in his effort to save her had also been badly burned and was unable to attend her funeral. His facial injuries required he stopped shaving. The ensuing beard now became the quintessential look that everyone remembers from pictures.

Devastated, he never fully recovered and sometimes resorted to laudanum and ether to ease the pain. He worried he would go insane and begged "not to be sent to an asylum" and noted that he was "inwardly bleeding to death". In the sonnet "The Cross of Snow" (1879), which he wrote eighteen years later he wrote:

"Such is the cross I wear upon my breast
These eighteen years, through all the changing scenes
And seasons, changeless since the day she died".

Longfellow spent several years translating Dante Alighieri's epic poem, The Divine Comedy. To aid him in perfecting the translation and reviewing proofs, he invited several friends to weekly meetings every Wednesday from 1864. This became known as the "Dante Club", and regulars included William Dean Howells, James Russell Lowell, Charles Eliot Norton and other occasional guests. The full three-volume translation was published in the spring of 1867, though Longfellow would continue to revise it. It was wildly popular and was re-printed four times in its first year.

By 1868, Longfellow's annual income was over a staggering $48,000.

Longfellow was also part of a group of Poets who became known as The Fireside Poets. The group included Longfellow, William Cullen Bryant, John Greenleaf Whittier, James Russell Lowell, and Oliver Wendell Holmes Snr. Occasionally Ralph Waldo Emerson is also placed among their number. The name "Fireside Poets" derives from poetry reading as a collective family entertainment of the times.

During the 1860s, Longfellow, still a committed abolitionist, also hoped for a coming together, a reconciliation, between the north and south after the dark days of the Civil War. When his son was wounded during the war, he wrote the poem "Christmas Bells", later the basis of the carol I Heard the Bells on Christmas Day.

In 1874, Samuel Cutler Ward helped him sell the poem "The Hanging of the Crane" to the New York Ledger for $3,000; it was the highest price ever paid for a poem. An astonishing sum. But Longfellow was worth it. His fame and audience were widespread and devoted.

Continuing in his hopes for a better and more united America he wrote in his journal in 1878: "I have only one desire; and that is for harmony, and a frank and honest understanding between North and South". Longfellow, despite his aversion to public speaking, took up an offer from Joshua Chamberlain to speak at his fiftieth reunion at Bowdoin College. Here he read the poem "Morituri Salutamus" so quietly that few could hear.

On August 22th, 1879, a female admirer who seemed to know little about his history, traveled to Longfellow's house in Cambridge and, unaware to whom she was speaking, asked Longfellow: "Is this the house where Longfellow was born?" Longfellow told her it was not. The visitor then asked if he had died here. "Not yet", he replied.

Much of Longfellow's work is recognized for its melody-like musicality. As he says, "what a writer asks of his reader is not so much to like as to listen".

Longfellow, like many others of the period, called for the development of high quality American literature. In his work, Kavanagh, a character says: "We want a national literature commensurate with our mountains and rivers... We want a national epic that shall correspond to the size of the country... We want a national drama in which scope shall be given to our gigantic ideas and to the unparalleled activity of our people... In a word, we want a national literature altogether shaggy and unshorn, that shall shake the earth, like a herd of buffaloes thundering over the prairies."

As a translator Longfellow was very impressive. His translation of Dante's The Divine Comedy became a requirement for those who wanted to be a part of high culture.

In 1874, Longfellow oversaw a 31-volume anthology called Poems of Places, collecting poems of several geographical locations; Europe, Asia, and the Arabian countries. It was a work of great educational endeavor but Emerson was disappointed and is said to have told Longfellow: "The world is expecting better things of you than this... You are wasting time that should be bestowed upon original production".

At this point in his life Longfellow could look back and see that his early collections, Voices of the Night and Ballads and Other Poems, had made him instantly popular. The New-Yorker called him "one of the very few in our time who has successfully aimed in putting poetry to its best and sweetest uses". The Southern Literary Messenger immediately put Longfellow "among the first of our American poets".

The rapidity with which American readers embraced Longfellow was unparalleled in publishing history in the United States. His popularity spread throughout Europe, his poems translated into Italian, French, German, and other languages.

Longfellow was the most popular poet of his day. As a friend once wrote to him, "no other poet was so fully recognized in his lifetime". Some of his works including "Paul Revere's Ride" and "The Song of Haiwatha" may have rewritten the facts but became essential parts of the American psyche and culture. He was so admired that on his 70th birthday in 1877 the atmosphere was that of a national holiday, with parades, speeches, and, of course, the reading of his poems.

Over the years, Longfellow's reputation came to include his personality; he was a gentle, placid, poetic soul. James Russell Lowell said, Longfellow had an "absolute sweetness, simplicity, and modesty". The reality was that Longfellow's life was much more difficult than was assumed. He suffered from neuralgia, which caused him constant pain, and poor eyesight. The difficulties of coping with the loss of two wives also took its toll. He was very quiet, reserved, and private; in later years, he became increasingly unsocial and avoided leaving home if he could.

In March 1882, Longfellow went to bed with severe stomach pain. He endured the pain for several days with the help of opium.

Henry Wadsworth Longfellow died, surrounded by family, on Friday, March 24th, 1882. He had been suffering from peritonitis.

He is buried with both of his wives at Mount Auburn Cemetery in Cambridge, Massachusetts. At Longfellow's funeral, his friend Ralph Waldo Emerson called him "a sweet and beautiful soul".

At the time of his death, his estate was valued at $356,320.

In 1884, Longfellow became the first non-British writer for whom a sculpted bust was placed in Poet's Corner of Westminster Abbey in London; he remains the sole American poet thus represented.

Henry Wadsworth Longfellow – A Concise Bibliography

Outre-Mer: A Pilgrimage Beyond the Sea (Travelogue) (1835)
Hyperion, a Romance (1839)
The Spanish Student. A Play in Three Acts (1843)
Evangeline: A Tale of Acadie (poem) (1847)
Kavanagh (1849)
The Golden Legend (poem) (1851)
The Song of Hiawatha (poem) (1855)
The New England Tragedies (1868)
The Divine Tragedy (1871)
Christus: A Mystery (1872)
Aftermath (poem) (1873)
The Arrow and the Song (poem)

Poetry Collections

Voices of the Night (1839)
Ballads & Other Poems (1841)
Poems on Slavery (1842)
The Belfry of Bruges & Other Poems (1845)
The Seaside and the Fireside (1850)
The Poetical Works of Henry Wadsworth Longfellow (1852)
The Courtship of Miles Standish & Other Poems (1858)
Tales of a Wayside Inn (1863)
Birds of Passage (1863)
Household Poems (1865)
Flower-de-Luce (1867)
Three Books of Song (1872)
The Masque of Pandora & Other Poems (1875)
Kéramos & Other Poems (1878)
Ultima Thule (1880)
In the Harbor (1882)

Michel Angelo: A Fragment (incomplete; published posthumously)

Coplas de Don Jorge Manrique (Translation from Spanish) (1833)
Dante's Divine Comedy (Translation) (1867)

Poets and Poetry of Europe (Translations) (1845)
The Waif (1845)
Poems of Places (1874)